Love: A Suspect Form
Heloise and Abelard

Love: A Suspect Form

Heloise and Abelard

Judith Infante

for
Francois de Berenx —

Judith Infante

Nov 2008

Shearsman Books
Exeter

First published in the United Kingdom in 2008 by
Shearsman Books Ltd
58 Velwell Road
Exeter EX4 4LD

www.shearsman.com

ISBN-13 978-1-905700-82-0

Contents

III

IV

To my daughters
Nora, Gabriela, and Juliet

A Visit to The Paraclete

Driving from Paris we have passed through countryside that in the twelfth century belonged to Count Thibault of Champagne. Early fall has muted the slightly undulant fields to buff and soft green; crops are in, agribusiness lulled. I catch the outlines of the ancient fortress and the church tower that crown Provins, where Abelard surely visited the count. Further on, outside Nogent-sur-Seine stand the distant twin stacks of nuclear reactors, then appears the cut-off for A16 and a sign to Le Paraclete.

Eight kilometres later we turn onto a narrow country road that was laid with small cobblestones hundreds of years before Europeans dreamed of the New World. It leads us past the outer wall of a large stone barn. (How elegant these ancient barns, their picturesque weight bespeaking a narrative remote from the frame structures of my North Carolina farm childhood.) Fast beside the barn where I can glimpse an assortment of farm machinery stands a red brick Regency-style house behind tall, emphatically closed wrought iron gates. Beyond appears another structure by a stream. This must be a mill; yes, there is the grindstone leaning against the building. And this stream is a rivulet that becomes the River Ardusson. The car bumps over an old culvert guiding the water towards the woods. It's still, almost oppressive. No animals in the fields, no people to be seen. Not far from town, but seeming isolated. Not quite deserted, but not inviting.

After his first trial for heresy in 1121, Abelard came here and built an oratory of mud and thatch. At the time it was a somewhat primitive area, but not the wilderness Heloise called it. Even then Champagne was intensely cultivated; the villages and monasteries in the area used every plot of land available. The gloomy trees beneath which we rattle along would be the product of land returned to forest. Over a rise, and the cobblestones stop in a clearing marked with stubble from a recent harvest. We turn back towards the silent buildings.

For five years I have been imagining this place as it must have been in the twelfth century. Abelard was here first; then Heloise, his pupil, his lover, mother of his son, his wife, fellow religious, and the first Abbess of the Order of The Paraclete.

For nearly nine hundred years the story of Heloise and Abelard has endured. It is spectacular in its most famous elements — love letters between a nun and monk, a secret marriage, a child lost to history. In popular imagination this is the story's chronology, but the events were reversed. As is usual with people's lives, things were complex.

Around 1117, the philosopher Peter Abelard taught at the newly established university in Paris. He was famous throughout Europe and, he tells us in his autobiography, believed himself "Philosopher of the World." Heloise (no one knows her family name), niece of a canon at Notre Dame, was his pupil. Reared in a convent near Paris she was brilliant and uncommonly educated for a young woman, known for her mastery of Latin rhetoric and her familiarity with the Roman classics. Her uncle employed Abelard to give her lessons. "Need I say more?" asks Abelard. Their affair resulted in the birth of a son whom she named Astralabe. Later they wed in a secret ceremony, but never lived together. The church had new requirements of celibacy for its teachers, especially for so conspicuous a master as Peter Abelard. In the hope he might retain his status and his pupils, Abelard insisted the marriage remain secret. For reasons not entirely clear, perhaps even to himself, he soon sent Heloise back to the convent of Argenteuil. Her uncle considered this to be abandonment and, in a semi-legal act of revenge, paid to have Abelard drugged and castrated. Very soon thereafter, in 1118, the lovers took religious orders, she at her husband's bidding. Thereafter they saw each other but on a few occasions.

As we turn from the field and head back towards the house, I tell Alexandre, my driver for the day, that I'll walk. I want to get closer to the low wall that extends from the mill across the culvert and along the road. Maybe I will be able to glimpse the obelisk that, according to the guidebook, marks the place where the couple once were buried. An obelisk: strange, Napoleonic tribute to medieval lovers and destroyed convent. Through a tangle of long-limbed ground vines, I reach the low wall topped by a wrought iron fence. I can hear the steady rush of water beneath the mill house. But I see only the red brick manse that is out of sync with any medieval expectations I had.

And what expectations can I have? What do I want to find here? Every poem, whatever the subject, is about the writer.

Several years ago a friend shared with me a poem she had written after visiting the tomb of Abelard and Heloise in the Père-Lachaise cemetery in Paris. Her poem led me to a line Abelard had written in one of his hymns: "Deep in thy grave with thee, happy to lie." I stood at a window in my favorite room of the home that I would soon leave forever. As I looked out on live oak trees and low mountains of the Texas Hill Country, I repeated to myself words of a twelfth-century French monk. That must have been the moment these poems began, cell by cell, word by many rejected word. What happens when two souls join, then part? Perhaps they can meet again, content with each other in some far spiritual hinterland. But what about the long interval of days, what shape might they take?

A life is about changing forms, Ovid tells us: metamorphosis. Ovid, author of scandalous love poetry and titillating myth narratives, was incongruously present in every scriptorium in the middle ages. Novices read him and copied out passages, supposedly for the fine examples of Latin usages. Sophisticated bishops quoted him at their tables. Surely they did not miss the parallel courses of myth and "real" life that they observed every day. After taking orders, Abelard and Heloise, teacher and student, lovers, husband and wife, parents, were changed into monk and nun, brother and sister, father and daughter, son and mother.

Loving souls severed from each other, willingly or reluctantly, must take up new identities. In some form they have to make their way in the world, working out their individual narratives. The reactions of Heloise and Abelard to their new roles were strikingly different.

As a monk Abelard was entirely committed to his vision

of God and Church, and he never ceased teaching and writing on the subject. For him, the use of one's rational faculties has a moral basis. Conscientious and informed reasoning leads to a more complete understanding of God: "By doubting", he wrote, "we come to inquiry and by inquiry we perceive the truth." Statements like this kept him in conflict with rival teachers and conservative elements in the Church. In 1121, three years after taking orders at the prestigious monastery of St. Denis, he was condemned as a heretic and his books were burned. Abelard himself could have been put to the flames. However, he had friends with influence, and soon he was granted permission to establish a small oratory in the region of Champagne. He named the chapel The Paraclete, a term which refers to the Holy Spirit as Comforter. Within a few years the oratory and its adjacent buildings were abandoned because Abelard was sent as Abbot to a remote and unruly monastery in Brittany. Ten years later he returned to Paris and was again a master at the university. Then in 1140 came his second trial and condemnation as a heretic. Once again he barely escaped execution. He was over sixty and weakened by an illness with symptoms that scholars speculate indicated Hodgkinson's disease; yet he was determined to appeal his case in Rome and he set out—walking. He never made it to Rome, but he did find refuge in the great Burgundian abbey of Cluny. He died there, perhaps within the year. Peter the Venerable, Abbot of Cluny, personally brought Abelard's body to The Paraclete for burial.

Heloise, on the other hand, entered the religious life with no vocation for it. Her heart remained in the hidden rooms of her romance. More than ten years after taking the veil, she revealed in letters to Abelard that daily she was consumed with longing for him and with resentment towards a God whom she held responsible for her husband's castration and her misery. Nonetheless, she was appointed Prioress of Argenteuil and held that post until the abbey was dissolved in 1129, when Abbot Suger claimed the land for St. Denis. The nuns at Argenteuil had to find other religious houses to take them in. At this point, with no family support and no one with influence to intercede for her,

Heloise was truly alone in the world. Apparently, no convent would accept her. Upon hearing of this, Abelard, who by then was in Brittany, asked for authority to establish Heloise and a few other nuns at the oratory of The Paraclete in Champagne. She was named Abbess of The Paraclete in 1131. Thirty-three years later on these grounds she died, having lived more than twenty years after Abelard's death.

At the time of her death she was universally respected for her administrative skills, her diplomacy, and her piety. What is not known is whether she ever ceased to think of herself as a hypocrite, someone wearing a habit of Christian submission over her true pagan Roman skin. If she was diligent in her duties, that virtue probably was derived as much from her readings of the Roman moralists such as Cicero as from her acceptance of monastic rule. No doubt, she also had a strong desire for personal accomplishment. We will never know if she considered The Paraclete, the shelter her husband deeded to her, as more than another form of on-going punishment.

And no one knows what Astralabe, the son left in Brittany, thought about his parents or what contact he might have had with them. It was not an age that valued the parent-child relationship, but it's hard to imagine that even in the middle ages abandoned children were not curious about their parents, and resentful. Even after he became a young man, it would have been difficult for him to overcome the barriers of church protocol and his parents' apparent self-absorption to initiate communication with them. What is known is scant: there exists a poem of advice attributed to Abelard which is dedicated to an Astralabe; and when Astralabe was about twenty, his mother wrote the kindly-disposed Peter the Venerable asking for a position as canon for her son. It is not known for certain what became of the request. Loose ends in a story.

Certainly the story suggested on the present grounds of The Paraclete is discontinuous and seems closed off to me. Though no fierce dogs run out at us, as had been predicted by another writer who had recently tried to visit, neither is there a clear view of the landmarks. I can see the back of a vaguely

Romanesque-style stucco chapel, but no obelisk, no evidence of a crypt. At this point Alexandre parks the car and walks through the arched gateway to the courtyard in front of the barn. After all, the tall iron gates are open here and, from the look of them, have been for centuries. I think, too, he has had enough of this woman who has come from Texas to such an odd place, then merely hovers around the edges.

He knocks at the door of what we presume is the caretaker's house; he is going to ask permission to see the obelisk. A youngish woman answers the door. She fits my image of unaffected French elegance—medium height, medium dark hair in a simple cut, her skin perfect without makeup. Her shirt and Bermudas are classic and her loafers slightly scuffed, as befits life in the country. Alexandre must be very well spoken because she becomes liltingly animated. I understand that she gives tours only in July and August, *Je regrette*. Now Alexandre earns his tip: But Madame has come all the way from Texas for research. She asks if I teach philosophy. Oh, no, Alexandre exclaims, Madame is a Poet! Writing about Heloise and Abelard! She exclaims in turn, *Ah! Une poète! Un moment.* She opens the door to her house, and out bursts Oliver, a black and white spaniel puppy ready for action. He adores everyone's shoes and wants to pee on them all; in fact he adores us so much he gets severely stepped upon at least twenty times in the next twenty minutes. We head to the grounds, Madame of the Farm explaining the ages of the various buildings, the difficulty of keeping just the right number of doves in the ancient dovecote, the play that was performed on the grounds two years ago.

She is the daughter-in-law of the owners of the manor and the land around it. She loves the farm life, and she loves the story of Abelard and Heloise. Her husband's family has lived here since shortly after the Revolution, when the Order of the Paraclete was dissolved and the convent vandalized, then sold. (A member of the Comédie-Française built the Regency mansion over the shell of the convent's priory.) By the time of the Revolution, the Paraclete was a large, prosperous enterprise with an aristocratic membership. Monks from nearby Benedictine monasteries were hired as laborers. It could not have been more unlike what Heloise found when she first came here.

There were a few crumbling buildings and nothing else. In his autobiography Abelard concedes that the first years were difficult for the nuns. There was hard physical labour to be performed, and the nuns had to do most of it themselves. This meant no time for Heloise, the high-born scholar, to read. However, as she swept floors or worked in the fields she might have been reminded of any number of ancient stories in which characters find themselves turned into beings alien from what they know of themselves. There was Io, the maiden turned into a white cow after being raped by Jove. And Heloise's story resonates with that of Atalanta: abandoned at birth and brought up in a sacred cave, she became famous for her swiftness in the races. However, she and her husband offended the goddess Cybele with their passion and were turned into lions, condemned eternally to pull her cart across the sky. There is little evidence left now of what Heloise's daily life would have been like in the twelfth century. The present chapel is a small replacement for the one destroyed in the Revolution. The obelisk beside it, like most obelisks, is unremarkable. It's supposed to stand on the spot where Heloise and Abelard were buried when their coffins were removed from the original crypt to drier ground. Ah, the crypt.

We walk down a slope to what looks like the mouth of a cave. The floor is paved with stone slabs, as are the walls. It's a dank, empty space where two coffins, encased in outer vaults, once lay side by side. The truth is, the bones of Heloise and Abelard have travelled. Four times they were moved within the precinct of The Paraclete itself. Just prior to the Revolution they were transferred for safety to a church in Nogent-sur-Seine, perhaps moved twice there. In 1800 they were taken to Paris and entombed in a museum, but finally came to rest in the company of other notables and celebrities, including Jim Morrison, at Père-Lachaise cemetery. Even today there always are bouquets and love poems tucked in the low wrought iron fence surrounding their elaborate marble tomb. Ironically, there commonly are mix-ups when remains are moved from tomb to tomb. No one knows for certain that the bones in Paris are actually theirs.

Our hostess, Alexandre, Oliver, and I peer into the dark little chamber. She repeats the famous legend: The lovers are buried together. When the lid of Abelard's coffin is lifted, he extends his arms to receive his true love. "Deep in thy grave with thee, happy to lie." I'm sure Heloise would not like this story. She was too much a child of Latin classics to be sentimental or morbid, and she wanted a life in the here and now.

Obligations are calling the charming Madame of the Farm. There's not a lot to see after all, in the way of buildings. But I really came to The Paraclete to learn what the water is like here, its colors, what creatures live on its banks. Tibault gave Abelard refuge on some boggy land; Heloise turned it into a prestigious institution that endured for six hundred years. Here was the home and the project for her life, both of which her husband gave to her. It was not the romanticized, high-minded life of the mind that she wanted. But, given her scholarly nature, her intelligence, and the time in which she lived, it was the best life available to her.

And the land was always here for her, waiting to give. At this point the Ardusson is a stream becoming a river, and above the mill, more of a pond. Quiet water, even as it falls over the small stone dam to the mill. Where we are standing, tall reeds form a buffer between the water and the crypt. Perfect duck habitat. On cue, a clutch of young mallards swims into the open. Across the water, a heron lifts. Ah!

Characters

Peter Abelard [Pierre Abélard]: c.1079–1142. Born at Le Pallet, near Nantes in Brittany. His parents apparently were minor nobility. His skill at teaching and argumentation made him one of the most famous thinkers of his day; but he also was a controversial figure, both for his philosophy/ theology and for the conduct of his personal life. His writings influenced the thought of later philosophers, including Thomas Aquinas.

Heloise [Héloïse]: c.1090–1163. Only her mother's name, Hersinde, is known. She was educated at the convent of Argenteuil and perhaps at the Cathedral of Notre-Dame. When she met Abelard, probably when she was in her mid-twenties, she was considered the most educated woman in France. In his autobiography Abelard refers to her as *adolescentia*, a term referring to an unmarried female between the ages of 14 and 30.

Peter Astralabe: c.1118. Sometimes spelled Astrolabe or Astrolabius. Son of Abelard and Heloise, he was left after his birth to be reared by Abelard's sister in Le Pallet. Nothing else definite is known about him. It is possible he is the same Canon Astralabe at the Nantes Cathedral in 1150 and/or the Abbot Astralabe of Hauterive in Fribourg in 1162.

Hersinde: Variously spelled Hersendis, or Hersint. Mother of Heloise. Nothing else definite is known about her. She is commemorated in the Necrology of The Paraclete on December 1, the Feast of Saint Eloi.

Fulbert: died c.1127. Uncle and guardian of Heloise. Apparently of a well-connected family, he was Canon of Notre-Dame in Paris. He was responsible for Abelard's castration. At the time castration was not an entirely illegal revenge upon a man who had dishonored a woman and her family.

(St.) Bernard of Clairvaux: c.1090–1153. An aristocrat from Burgundy, he was Abbot of the Cistercian monastery of

Clairvaux. An immensely influential churchman, writer, and preacher, he promoted the Second Crusade. At Abelard's trial for heresy at Sens in 1140, Bernard was the prosecutor.

Peter the Venerable: c.1092–1156. Also from Burgundy, Peter was said to be the most powerful figure in the church after the Pope. He was Abbot at the great monastery of Cluny, and often in dispute with Bernard of Clairvaux. After the Council of Sens, Peter gave Abelard shelter, professed him a monk of Cluny, and readmitted him to "apostolic grace."

Ovid: 43 BCE–17 CE. Publius Ovidius Naso, a Roman poet. His work was widely read in the middle ages, especially his interpretations of classical myths. Despite his sophisticated treatment of sexuality, Ovid's work was used as a standard for Latin composition in church schools. In 08 CE he was banished to a remote corner of the Roman Empire, and he died there nine years later.

Atalanta: A figure from classical mythology. She was abandoned by her father, King Iasus, but the goddess Artemis in the guise of a bear rescued Atalanta, and raised her in the wild. When she became famous as a hunter and runner, her father reclaimed her. Her great beauty inspired men to race against her for her hand, but she always won. Hippomenes appealed to Aphrodite, who distracted Atalanta by tossing golden apples in her path during their race. Later the couple offended both Aphrodite and Cybele and were turned into lions.

The cause is hidden, but the power known.

Ovid, *The Metamorphoses,* IV

Now I shall tell of things that change, new being
Out of old . . .

Ovid, *The Metamorphoses*, Book I

I will gladly do my best to obtain a prebend in one of the great churches for your [son] Astralabe, who is also ours for your sake.

Letter 168, Peter the Venerable, to Heloise

O Atalanta . . . yet alive, you shall lose all that is yours, and never get away.

Ovid, *The Metamorphoses*, Book X

Astralabe: Master of Script
(An abbey school on the coast of Brittany, around 1140)

These adolescents accept they have missed The Age of Gold, when no beast, no man was base. What's more, they suspect our abbey cowers at the edge of the world in a late, dark time. (The roar you hear is the ocean flingling salt and grit against our walls.)

Gifts to God and obedient, the boys wrap chilblained fingers round their quills and copy phrases from Ovid. The poet of love suffers a new exile, to church scriptoriums all over Christendom.

Feigning deafness to love meter and chill to Atalanta who wears but ankle ribbons as she races down the vellum page, they hold square-nib pens at sharp angles. In Carolingian letters they shape the oracle's warning:

Lay not with man! Ascender, descender, ligature of characters, plot demands monition be forgot.

A student clears his nose in his soured sleeve; others snigger at the temple coupling. They have theories why I often assign this tale. One grins, his stained finger taps *amor's* urgent beat. (Ink pot falls, ocean pummels its own rhythm.)

Young ignorance moves me, simple minds eager to writhe on sacred floors, spell-struck and naked. As if sex is the point.

O what Powers—lusty gifts and sudden offense! A maiden's skin erupts in laurel runnels, gentle twigs like fingers snap when They send a godly wind. A youth fondling his sister's white arm is rebuffed by a raven's wing. Claws bedded in coarse pelt stroke a lover's face.

Atalanta was turned to lion, my mother made nun.
Cybele, one ancient conjurer was called.
I'm loathe to name the other.

. . . indeed, [the Lord] has you much in mind, for by a kind of holy pres-
age of his name, he marked you out to be especially his when he named
you Heloise, after his own name Elohim.
　　Letter 4, Abelard to Heloise

Mother House

(Abbey of Ste. Marie of Argenteuil)

Heloise—derived from Elohim—therefore,
dedicated to God, therefore,
an offering

In the shaft of afternoon Heloise,
a child upon her pallet, curves
into a bell. As insects drone,
light glides along the wall and lures

her with arms warm and entwining.
Dust motes spiral and rise along
a ladder lit to heaven. And they sing.
She thinks she remembers this song

which calls to another. Under her tongue
the response quivers. She wants to touch
the phantom voice. Sing with it. But not one
thing can she hold. To clutch

afternoon light leaves you cold. Night will come
and time beats a loud, empty drum.

Here is the story from Arkadia about Atalanta. At birth her father exposed
her. The child was under sentence of death, but shortly afterwards arrived
a bear . . .breasts bulging and weighed down with milk.
  Aelian, Historical Miscellany, 13.1

Ordinary Affair
  (Parthenian Hill, Archaic time)

No god holds Iasus accountable. And the infants,
debris of inopportune couplings, after-thoughts

and fragments scattered about in the rich spring grasses,
what does he owe them? He's not accountable

if some whimper. Not accountable for small skulls
like rocks under his feet, for dirty strings of flesh,

the vultures overhead. Not accountable for this
inconvenient daughter, though he tugs a corner

of the swaddling cloth to cover her perfect reddened
face. (The noon sun is hard.) Not accountable

if a slave trader loiters nearby hoping
for viable goods. Iasus thinks to make

an offering. But who gathers up the abandoned,
who carries them through the dark to eternal

chambers? He lays the infant Atalanta near
a vertebrae necklace and newly blossoming

wild flowers (he's high born and doesn't bother with
their names). The sun beats down exactly as it did

yesterday and as it will long after this child
drops from his memory's horizon. There's

flesh smell and hunting in the air. On a whim
he makes invocation to Artemis, goddess

of hunt and midwives. (A day like others.)
As Iasus turns away his daughter soundlessly

rolls down the hill's slight incline. As if some hand
guides her, she misses any stone or cadaver

that might stop her or snag the slow unwinding
cloths. Her father doesn't turn to see his child

lying at the bottom of the hill naked, limbs
flailing, unfortunate gender exposed. And why

should he look back—it's an ordinary affair,
an ordinary day. Careless man. He should know

every time is a remarkable time. A Presence
watches, and today She wears the pelt of a bear.

Perhaps you've heard the legend of a girl . . . who could outrun all
human kind, or girls or men.
Ovid, *The Metamorphoses*, Book X

A gift for letters is so rare in a woman—
Peter Abelard, *Historia Calamitatum*

Game
(Abbey of Ste. Marie of Argenteuil)

Heloise sucks hard on mythology's teat
and the bear's milk goes down fatty and sweet.

It's a heady infusion, a flex of greater thirst.
Soon hunters stop by the lair to tutor. She envies first

their tight dialectics, muscled declensions. Oracles
clad in black outfit her in Latin. Close to the pinnacle

of the *trivium* she stands. She makes herself a name.
And that's how she's turned into fleet-thinking game.

Iasus, delighted by her success . . . had grown impatient for the race to start.
Ovid, *The Metamorphoses, Book X*

Fulbert . . . was always ambitious to further his niece's education.
Peter Abelard, *Historia Calamitatum*

Heloise: Brought to Paris

1.Coffers
(Abbey of Ste. Marie of Argenteuil)

Trunks line the storage room wall, puzzles
with a past. Each holds a shift laid out
on crushed myrtle leaves, husks
we wore in an outer chamber
the day they blessed us and peeled
family away. My own mystery weighs
too much for its size and light
fabric. Who sewed it, who chose
the mulberry color? The sleeves reach as far
as the distance might be around
a mother's waist. My mother,
I'm told, gone to Jerusalem.

2. Dress
(Canon Fulbert's residence,
Close of Notre Dame, Paris)

Colour of plum and leaf-brown
shawl to cover it,

the dress I wore
when I entered my uncle's house.

Bits of learning and a body
whose meaning no one had taught me,

I was singular fruit
brought to Paris in a cart.

Hippomenes looked at Atalanta, and said
"Why play at honour against slow-footed fools?
Come, set your pace with mine."

Ovid, *The Metamorphoses*, X

*I had not quite passed the bounds of youth and reached early manhood
when I knew of your name and reputation.*
     Letter 115, Peter the Venerable, to Heloise

*I considered all the usual attractions for a lover and decided she was the
one to bring to my bed.*
     Peter Abelard, *Historia Calamitatum*

Reputation
     (Canon Fulbert's residence,
     Close of Notre Dame, Paris)

Fulbert who had carried her swaddled
in name and donations to the nuns
now opens his door for her. The small world

that is Paris wonders at nature
so deformed: a female given to learned
argument. It's a show. Bishops call her

daughter, gift her with rare books (she prefers
the pagan writers). Students bribe
her servants for a glimpse (it's rumored

her hair's uncovered—it's candle flare
or midnight, it's honey). Oblates pledged
to walled lives whisper her name beneath

their cowls, *Heloise.* There must be a plan:
no man of repute will have a wife
reading at books. Nor any husband, save

Christ. Does she want an abbey for her
own—library with a hundred tomes?
Now that the arc of her fame outruns

all thinkers in France, save one, he comes
to sup. "Philosopher of the World,"
he plans to unravel the mystery of her hair.

*I came to an arrangement with her uncle, whereby he should take me
into his house . . . he gave me complete charge over the girl.*
Peter Abelard, *Historia calamitatum*

Heloise: Lesson
(Canon Fulbert's residence,
Close of Notre Dame, Paris)

vellum from a goat's skin
bound into books

quills and ink on a table
first lesson

at midnight listen
my master climbs the stair

a mother might have taught me
the signs of a snare

who can tutor me now
in the art of breaking free

I could devote all the leisure time left me by my school to teaching her day and night, and if I found her idle I was to punish her severely
Peter Abelard, *Historia calamitatum*

Strix

(Canon Fulbert's residence,
Close of Notre Dame, Paris)

Elsewhere in the house her uncle
opens his chamber window to a breeze
lifting from the river. He believes
it is he who in this spider dwelling
has woven the tremulous net named
Heloise. As the philosopher's footfalls pass
his door and ascend towards the girl
Fulbert feels the vibrations of fame.

He has baited the net with fatty candles
that sputter and smoke on her study table, the soft
falling open of a tome. Tonight
passage to knowing is irresistible.
The startled cry pierces his thick
heart. *Strix*, he tells himself: owl.
Owl by the river has found his mark.

Need I say more?
Peter Abelard, *Historia calamitatum*

Heloise: Transported Measure
(Canon Fulbert's residence,
Close of Notre Dame, Paris)

Each time the master crossed my threshold,
he changed. I sat at the oak table behind
a fortress of books and witnessed

France's greatest mind coil into Ovid's
dark python of desire. "Read the pagan's
tales," he had assigned, "for the elegant

syntax, how he moves the narrative on."
Not so young, Abelard, nor smooth-skinned,
not lithe like the beauties Phoebus

loved. But his wit was known. His hand,
nails curved like a raptor's, trembled
above mine when he pointed to a phrase.

My first touch of wanting. Io ran but great
Jove's lust was quicker. *Nor am I
a common god . . . oh do not flee from me!*

Beneath my master's comely learning
moans and pants another creature. And isn't
Abelard a great man? The burning god

also wounded Io. His heavy mouth
commanded, *Obey*. Ink-stained
fingers kneaded and writhed, instructing.

Men write of these moments in transported
measure. My own lover held
a mirror to my bloodless face, bleeding

lips. I saw only a veil-like skin lost.
When Io looked for herself in a stream,
a milky white cow bellowed back.
Jove remained Jove.

I [Aphrodite] held three golden apples in my hands / Invisible to all but Hippomenes. / I gave him instructions how to use them.
Ovid, *The Metamorphoses*, X

An equal to an equal . . . whatever a lover gives to a lover.
Letter 81, Woman to Man, *The Lost Love Letters*

Golden

Though living, you will lose yourself.
Oracles and old nuns see

how this race will end. But beauty
does not want a safe wool habit,

the wealth of her hair cropped. Beauty
wants the race, accepts the taunt.

Three times she stops, pretending
desire for Aphrodite's trinkets.

(Her opponent, somewhat famous
and older, needs to catch his breath).

This is her win, her glamorous loss—
silvery ribbons that tossed and glittered

behind her, acquire new lustre,
tinted by conquest and dust.

To my very beloved, and to confess the truth, very skilled in love . . .
Letter 81, Woman to Man, *The Lost Love Letters*

Heloise: Only Morning Ever

Morning light covers us better
than cotton or linen. Pillows
are kind. We are words
compounded to one.
There's just this room, curtains
rising and falling like breath revealing
speech. Your skin is the secret
of my skin.

This is the only morning
that ever was. With a single word I touch
the light that creates
each object on the table,
this love-ache
when I walk. If I should utter
the name of that heat
which embraces me
which does not leave me,
we would fall from here to the world.

Heloise: Sun
(Paris)

Of women, I am poetry,
sun beyond metaphor,
at night, the pole star.
And morning rises with my
unfolding. Oh, my lover
sings with more cunning,
even, than he reasons.
Who does not know my name?

Though I choose my tunic
and sleeves with care,
it is idle vanity. For he dresses me
in verse that gilds the meanest
street pond and burnishes
the tanner's sign. My passage
through the streets illumes
his art. Oh, ballad

of me! Leaning on their draped
window sills, great ladies
marvel at my light. Housewives
who carry purses on their belts
and women running market stalls

remark my trajectory.
From bath house doorways,
the loose-robed girls laugh
at my fortune. More brilliant

than a queen's gold circlet,
this song of me, verse
and meter composed in stealth
and secret midnight room.
Helios, blinding
source of my mortal god's day.
This song of me!

To avert suspicion I sometimes struck her, but these blows were prompted by love and tender feeling rather than anger and irritation, and were sweeter than any balm could be.

Peter Abelard, *Historia calamitatum*

Master of Logic

If the world of thought is one body, infinitely open,
she accepts that condition.

If spirits are three,
they enter through flesh, word, and potion.

If bleeding is prescribed for unfortunate humours,
she'll deny melancholy.

If he wants "no stage of lovemaking untried," or if days are holy,
words bend her to their ends.

If for a night of love, a beating makes it longer,
she'll choose that potion, and wholly.

And through the glass window shines the sun. / How should I love and I
so young?

Anonymous, *The Bride's Song*

. . . yea, I should not be despised / I would lead thee and bring thee /
into my mother's house / who would instruct me.

Song of Solomon 8.2

Heloise: Three Versions of My Conception

She is the only one of her mother. / She is the choice one of her that bare
her.

Song of Solomon 6.9

1.
Hersinde my mother
of the gold-flecked
bridal veil

whose own mother met
the wedding guests

she who was led, still sipping claret
from a silver goblet,
to the chamber prepared

who felt from the hall below a drum throb
and against an unseen hand
the rattle of a tambourine

then whose bare arms received the embroidered shift
whose breath rose towards the bed's canopy

and heard on the other side of the closed door
a final toast to her maiden self

The Lady Hersinde who was pearl
was jasmine flower upon the bridegroom's pillow
whose petals were untouched

who found his beard aromatic cedar
who saw herself a comely dove in his dark dove's gaze

Hersinde who received the bridegroom
in her mother's chamber
then watched him unfurl the emblazoned sheet
before her kinsmen

who had allowed him to lay his name upon her

. . . but my own vineyard have I not kept."
Song of Solomon I.6

2.
Hersinde my mother
who heard her kin at her heels
as she fled to meet him

whose skirts were hiked
in a shed musky
with animal sweat and bat dung
she whose breath was a small drum

who was a small mouse in his falcon eye

she with leaves and grass in her hair
a dusty hand print on her back
the smooth-skinned pear too easily plucked

who looked for him in the streets
and heard men laughing from a doorway
who heard the thief's untuned lute
and knew it was her name

whose single bed was a pallet beneath
attic beams of a dishonoured house
who touched herself even
as she thought of the shadow fallen
across her mother's empty room

Hersinde whose dowry
was a handful of gold
and a swollen secret

and no chevalier to take it

Thou hast ravished my heart, my sister, my spouse.
        Song of Solomon 4.9

3.
Hersinde with two soft swellings
like fledgling doves

whose brother gave her gifts
with their same initial
small items tied with silk
knotted like the cords
in her throat and belly

she who learned to hide for him
and not be found
who pulled back
the covers of her bed

he knotted her slippery hair
in his heavy fist and swore
her beating heart called him down
that long corridor of their childhood

the fact her heart beat

Hersinde who pulled back the covers for death
and called herself blessed

Above all, we want you to decide what we ought to do about reading the
Gospel in the Night Office. It seems to us hazardous if priests and deacons,
who should perform the reading, are allowed among us at such hours.
Letter 5, Heloise to Peter Abelard

Hersinde: My Version
(Abbey of St. Eloi, Ile de Cité, Paris, c.1095)

Bells for the Night Office announce
the secret. Our chaplain draws near.
When I have counted fifteen beads
he will arrive. All is prepared.

It was Ascension Day, the great
procession, when first my eyes fixed
upon him. When he gazed back,
I had been chosen. His brother priests,

familiar with my confessions,
gave him clues. But the sins were false.
Once I had seen his mouth in song,
I made a plan. Walls are porous,

visits legitimate. Evenings
he reads us gospel. Now the last
bead falls, the passage to chapel
is lit by chant. He knows my door.

The service ended, he will wait,
bridegroom, in the dark for silence.
All is prepared. Moon for mirror
and candle, I unbind my hair.
My sisters breathe *Jubilate!*

Heloise: Bead

Occulted bead of blood and humours,
Inside my cauldron spiralling your dream,

Listen!
I'm tapping the wall of your watery cave!

Small ink dot,
Hold fast.

Star burrowed in the dark,
Pearling pulsation,
Unreadable cipher,

Innocent sword,
Spoiler angel,
How will I shelter you?

Small ink dot,
Innocent sword,
Hold fast!

I removed her secretly and sent her straight to my own country . . . If
[her uncle] killed me or did me personal injury, there was the danger his
beloved niece would suffer for it.
                Peter Abelard, Historia calamitatum

Heloise: Journey
(from Paris to Le Pallet, Brittany)

1.
For the journey he gave me—first,
the command to go. For my safety. Then,
his servant to escort me, and strong
horses. For quick dispatch. He gave me clothes,
a black habit and nun's veil. For disguise,
he said, and further safety. Sincere, passionate
kisses. For persuasion. A prayer for health,
mine. A purse with money, in the servant's care.
(I begged for books to read in Brittany.)
More kisses. Slap to the rump of my mare.

2.
I stopped counting days after five. The hours
sloughed away in flakes of skin. Beneath
the wool cloak and false veil sweat
insinuated briars and creeping insects, a worm
burrowed at my waist. Even in afternoon rain.
The servant cursed all day. Our fine horses
walked at drudge's pace because
outside Paris the argument came to me:
A—A day of galloping is one remedy.
B—My master instructs me to ride hard to Brittany

(Not one prayer for the child!).
Therefore—My horse walks to Brittany.

3.

At the inn a garlic-scented woman
who shared the women's bed offered
love to a nun. The servant
refused me an extra jug of milk.
He wanted to desert, but my life
fell upon him.

There was afternoon thunder.
There was hail pounding my body. Ice stung
my face. The horses reared. I turned
away from Brittany, back to my chamber,
my writing table, fresh brew,
warm words for a prodigal.
My horse flew towards Paris.
Horse's mane in hand, I decided
Pegasus should be the babe's
Godfather, for Great Jove Abelard
is his sire.
                    It could not have been
a mile before my jailer overtook us.
"Ignorant woman."

There she stayed with my sister until she gave birth to a boy, whom she
called Astralabe.

Peter Abelard, Historia calamitatum

. . . and in that house, allow to be born neither the misshapen of limb,
nor the lame; nor the deaf and speechless nor any possessed by a devil.

Anonymous, Seinte Marharete: Meiden ant Martyr

Heloise: Birth at Le Pallet

(Le Pallet, Brittany, c.1118)

1.

A son—because I never failed
to sleep on my right. Born under Mars,
he will be irascible. I give him
Helios of learning and infamy.

Is he deformed? Is his foot club, or upper lip split,
palate too thick for song, no fingers to hold a quill?
For his father and I violated Sabbath. And Lent, as well;
are his limbs a starveling's or fat to burst?
And the fine black hairs that cover him
like a cub? We explored many configurations,
for all knowledge is God.

Is his father alive? Yes, I think, and not
in jail. For the same rude servant
delivered a money pouch here,
but not to me. Gold coins have not
bought clean rushes for my floor,
nor embroidered sheets on which a new mother
should lie, nor linen to swaddle the child.
Where is the upright woman to nurse him, as befits

who I am? The rose oil for her breasts?
No cupboard in this room displays
his family's wealth, my one book is gone.
No plates of silver with sugared fruits,
no sweets, no visitors to admire
his infant perfection. Will he go blind?
I failed to see the wages of a public love.

2.

When pain knotted my screams into an owl's
screech they loosened my hair. To inspire
my channel gates, doors and windows
were flung open. But the child,
wrapped in his last moments of true shelter,
resisted my need. Finally, I opened
my eyes and saw the sky—animate and black.
How very near the stars approach if called.
In a great measured wave he came.
So clear was heaven then, I named him Astralabe.

Moreover, to conciliate him [Fulbert] further, I offered him
satisfaction in a form he never could have hoped for: I would marry
the girl I had wronged.

Peter Abelard, *Historia calamitatum*

Astralabe: My Father Proposes Marriage

Irreparable damage demands equal loss.
A virgin has been corrupted, therefore:
   My father's eyes can be expunged, for the first violation of her.
   And his testes which incited the lust.

There has been treason, deception of a host.
There has been abduction, which implies force.
And he has offered no proof that my mother lives, therefore:
   More castration and blinding, if not hanging.
Such is the romance that shapes Peter Abelard's thoughts as he
rides to Le Pallet.

Merely days old am I, or weeks, or months, when he snatches
her away a second time. He's not a monk yet, and he's proud
of his horses and style of riding (heel deep into the flank, like
rustic gentry). In my uncle's meagre courtyard he makes a
clatter. All eyes are on the money bag at his belt.

What was the sound of my father's laugh—was it deep, did he
cackle? What did Heloise hear that never failed to draw her?

   "Down on my knees before Fulbert, I on my knees! Just
   another poor man, I told him, duped by Eve's unfortunate
   gender, her serpent weakness.

You will curve back into your chamber, write letters again. Every day the wax tablet delivered to my door, your perfect Latin love, beeswax secrets that melt my immortal soul! O back to Paris!

Small love. I need you in Paris, ergo, Philosophy needs you in Paris. And!—I will marry you!"

My mother knows about Cicero and Ovid, Lucan and Virgil. She aspires to Roman Concubinage to High Learning (ergo, my father). She wants a house of her own for the two of us. She believes in sweet conjugal meetings, educated visitors. At least two servants.

As they speak, the meteor of my father's career is sinking like a stone in polluted water. Students desert his classes. Daily he swears to her uncle that she is not dead. In the taverns young wits toss about the one man's many names—World's Philosopher. Licker of Lard. Arch Poet. Murderer.

Does he even look at me, Impediment with the Laughable Name? Does she thrust me to him—for a brief time, I believe, she was in love with me. Oh, but a baby won't keep my father out of jail, his eyes from the hot iron, his privates from the knife, won't lift the noose from his neck. But he believes that marriage will.

Now his purse falls opens. Now there's money to hire a sweet girl to nurse me, there are coins for my godfathers, deposit for my board. See how he holds out the reins of the horse she'll ride. For one moment she stands her ground, even as it slips from beneath her. More coins for the nurse, my mother insists, meat and cream for her diet, new straw for her bed. For the breasts, oils of lavender and three varieties of rose. To make my nature loving and mild.

But the wench my aunt employs is an onion eater, and to clean her breasts she's given a paste of salt and rue.

. . . justice should weigh not what was done but the spirit in which it was done.

    Letter 1, Heloise to Peter Abelard

Heloise: Married
    (A private chapel near Notre Dame, Paris)

A proper ceremony requires
daylight, thus in darkness

he meets me at the altar. With
no word or glance

we wait for dawn's
anaemic ray. Requisite

the witnesses, furtive
the priest. Fornicator

in philosophy's bed, I was
Helios, Ascending Star. Wife

is my falling. No ring. Could
not we be given

days entire, a dwelling,
front doorway? Full

light? Child
at breast? Priest

blesses us. We thank
God. My husband bows,

Deny this act. Still high
philosopher among

celibates, he leaves
to his breakfast. Bearing

new deceit, I return
to my uncle's house.

. . . and we did not see each other any more except very occasionally and secretly, concealing to the uttermost what we had done.
    Peter Abelard, *Historia Calamitatum*

Heloise: Once Sun
   (Paris)

like dung this secret
is the smear all
know me by

"common street dust
where is she running to
what assignment"

such mean
rooms and
measured time

he allots to me
once luna
once meridian

what term
fits me now
proof in bruises

hidden by sleeves
and skirt
proof in luck

such fame
would marry
this girl of no father

mother of bastard
wife of no husband

vain girl

. . . how great are the obstacles, the burdens, and the dangers in which marriage abounds.
  Peter Abelard, *Theologia Christiana*

Between Scylla and Charybdis

letters of the word lover
visible still on the mind's page
romantic ghosts not quite buried
              but writ over
        by a hard new word
        a scar
                        wife

bills accumulate
          her uncle wants it public
                  legitimate
          reputations are on the wrack
                          bruises appear
                  letters of the word wrath

        and their bodies call
  one to the other
        re-write
          the word lover

                          bruises on the mind's page
          ghosts appear
                  public and callosed

romance buried yet visible

wrath is

quick

bruises visible and public

reputations writ over

she must be sheltered

on the page forms another word

the nuns think him callous
yet sell him a robe
here reputations dress in black

and lover is writ as Ghost

After our marriage, when you were living in the cloister with the nuns at
Argenteuil and I came one day to visit you privately . . .
    Letter 4, Peter Abelard to Heloise

Heloise: Afternoon Light
    (Abbey of Ste. Marie of Argenteuil)

1.
Nones, the ninth hour, and afternoon work
drones on. In the field sickles lift
and fall. Chaff clouds the air.
Ovid preferred afternoon
love making, for the marriage
wrought of light and nakedness.

My lover visits and slow
we circle paths among parterres of herbs,
some bitter, and roses. We breathe
barely. A dram of scent requires
a thousand rose petals. I would crush more.

Holding his cloak before him like a canopy
sheltering the holy ark, he tries to conceal
his want. In this stillness
I hear a bell, or believe I do.
So in preparation for a nun's life,
I take pity and lead him inside.

2.

In the refectory bare floor and tables,
Holy Mother to one side in a shaft of light.
I move to his moving, this is not

what he wants. ("We could exchange letters!")
Afternoon light is lovely on flesh, but we are blind
and wear too many clothes.

Blindly he moves, this is not
what he wants. For the last time he falls
to the afternoon, which is what he wants.

I lost my temper at his ingratitude / And planned . . . / To make
Hippomenes and his bride a common case.
    Ovid, *The Metamorphosis*, X

Grotto
  (Archaic time)

They don't wonder why the noon's pulse roars
so loud and close, nor who chose this road
that ends at a shrine's ancient lips. As the air

thickens, a singular charge races from his
fingers to her shoulder. When she turns
to him it flares and returns. The world

vibrates to one note. At the grotto entry
some hand has draped boughs of pine,
sacred to a more cruel age. Wanting

to be pulled aside, the pungent needles
quiver in the still. Who lifts the branches,
then lets them fall behind after guiding

the lovers in? To enter is to abandon light.
They stand touching but almost blind, dim
to each other. The chamber has been

readied with quiet susurrus of water
along the walls, and beneath their feet
smooth stone pavers. He asks her to lie

upon them and she does. So commanding
is the force about them, the poet tells us,
that even the ancestral gods, images long

sheltered in thick cavernous dusk—snakes
in eternal coupling, voracious Priapus,
great-bellied women—avert their faces.

Now the love goddess has nothing left
to do, for Great Mother Cybele sees
the mortals writhing on her sacred

floor. In holy rage She presses hard
one bejewelled foot upon their conjoined
bodies. A jolt, and suddenly each gasps

as the other's sleek enveloping becomes
a weight. Abrasive tongues, alien fangs
assault their numbing lips. Pliable flesh

coarsens to rough pelt, nerve endings
shudder. When she tries to speak, an earthquake
gathers in her throat. Huge eyes aflame,

she realizes this maw reflecting hers
belongs to the man Aphrodite favoured.
He wants to caress her disappearing face,

but claws are not for tenderness. Some force
speaks, and, averting their eyes from the horror
the other mirrors, they stand. Cybele's

burnished halters fall upon them and lock.
The goddess snaps the reins. Their great paws
test the feel of lion pads on the stone floor

where moments before they lay. *Penance!*
chides the goddess. Their astral course is set.
Penance! as she drives them back into light.

Yet for her service, thoughtful Cybele
put bits between their teeth and drove them smartly.

Ovid, *The Metamorphoses*, X

And so it was wholly just and merciful . . . for me to be reduced in that part
of my body which was the seat of lust and sole reason for those desires.
  Letter 4, Peter Abelard to Heloise

Astralabe: My Father's Names

Known for razor-like lectures, the ease with which he cuts
into any competing arguments, my father, for the sake of
illustration, calls himself Jester. Jester in a Jig. Jester Keeping
at Play Propositions for Lady Logic.

"And what" he famously asks, "is the substance of a man?" Brags
his substance is like David. I say his heart is Goliath. He claims
to have grace and youth and form. His name translates to Licker
of Lard. More real than the category Man, says Abelard, is he.
One and the same as the category Philosopher.

Some call him Rhinoceros, others Black Unicorn in the Lap
of a Virgin. He proposes that Peter loves his girl. Proposes
my mother remain in the convent. Proposes I stay forever in
Brittany. Proposes his life as it was before her silken cords.

Traitor, says her uncle. Defiler, says a law rarely applied.

For my father, law was executed with powder slipped into his
wine and with a wink for my mother's kin as his servant opened
the door.

Quick knife alters the substance of a man.
Cleanly removes the name of Lover.
Fallen Creature now, Abelard.
Apprentice Husband to Spirit.

Heloise had already agreed to take the veil in obedience to my wishes and entered a convent.

Peter Abelard, *Historia calamitatum*

Abelard: Suspect Form
(Abbey of Ste. Marie of Argenteuil)

I am severed from the One who burns me.
(He wants no offering whose testicles are cut
or bruised or torn). I am less than a healthy goat.

Yet she weeps. (Knowing I stand here in shadow
to see her veiling?) Familiar with the classics,
she addresses this wrong with a fitting quote—

Noble husband, too great for me to wed . . .
But was I not wronged first? Was I not
captive? Was she not changeable?

Her serpent body, thrilling object, turned
ordinary on me. Her sweet belly betrayed
our love, swelling into a womb.

Did she not invert the order of things?
Unknown to myself, like a drunken student
I forgot philosophy and composed love poems.

And the second wrong also was done upon me,
and has made me unwhole before the world.
(Beneath my windows the common people gawked.)

Was it my fate to bend that lofty head?
Enough of tragedy, it's a suspect form. By pain
God reveals His Design and comforts us!

Alone she stands at the altar, newly virgin
for Christ. Another wedding blacker than the first.
Now claim your due and see me gladly pay.

Praise the knife—I'm freed from more begot.
The bishop trembles his blessing over my wife.
Praise her veil—I'm spared any rival but God.

That what you have suffered in the body for a passing hour, I may suffer in
anguish of soul throughout my life, as I deserve.
   Letter 3, Heloise to Peter Abelard

So we both put on the religious habit, I in the Abbey of St. Denis and she
in the Convent of Argenteuil.
   Peter Abelard, *Historia calamitatum*

Consecration
   (Abbey of Ste. Marie of Argenteuil)

No one will look at him,
yet not one person is unaware
of the famous absence
he bears. The thought
of his wound
is larger than this chapel
where a woman,
pale and quoting Latin,
is disappearing
into the black robe he bought her.

And so when our baby son was born we entrusted him to my sister's
care . . .
    Peter Abelard, *Historia calamitatum*

She knew I would be utterly an orphan with no one . . . to give me the
loving care a little child needs at such an age.
    Guibert of Nogent, *Memoirs*

Astralabe: Stars

Stars are droplets of milk streaming from a goddess breast.
And I tell you, the orphan's mouth always dreams.
Distance unnameable yawns between me and the burning orbs.
My given star, isolate as hers.

. . . justice should weigh not what was done but the spirit in which it was done.

Letter 1, Heloise to Peter Abelard

Accounts

(Abbey of Ste. Marie de Argenteuil)

Numbers in declension down the page:
twig brooms reconciled with prayers for patrons
mumbled, firewood paid for with eggs

plucked from beneath a hen. Coffers
hoarding coins, and orchards
pledged, equal a new daughter's

black wedding shroud. Each bride
a cipher who has years to sort
debts from her credit, which is a braid

cropped then sold in town. Names laid
inside a tomb balance candles with a dowry.
The prioress stops at her own *dot*, paid

by an impatient man. In heaven and below, God
judges and writes off "Intention" with zero.

Behold now, how good and joyful a thing it is, for brethren to dwell together in unity!
    Psalms 133.1

Heloise: Compline

each night a different one prays
sky an over-turned cup

the hour swings to black
throws us onto its cots

low partition on either side
nocturnal rattle and snore

through the chinks above us
hard stars glint at heaven's core

pallet boards scrape my shoulder blades
one breath our allotment of space

He shall cover thee with his feathers and under his wings shalt thou trust.
Psalms 91.4

Heloise: Vigils

what is it
leaps to my cot
treads me
with five-fingered paws

who am I
can't shake
it off

every night the rough tongue
plays with me
I wear
the rasp of its breath

who am I

quiver of bone
and consent

Blessed are those that are undefiled in the way.
    Psalms 119.1

Heloise: Prime

I wake, morning, wound in my one dream.
Dreaming I wake in my lover's bed.

What to sing, dawn, as I rise in old clothes and take up my stone?
Stone, morning, heavy as an infant lost.

Love buried his arrows beneath this parchment wrap of bones.
Love keeps me bound in his bloody rags.

Hear how I sing, dawn, sing with a clotted heart.
With a clotted heart, dawn, singing my wound!

After the treatise began to please everyone, as it seemed to answer all the
questions on the subject, my rivals convened a Council against me.
    Peter Abelard, *Historia calamitatum*

On the Unity and Trinity of God
(First trial of Abelard for heresy, Soissons, 1121)

1.
To explain The Trinity
Hildegard sees three women inside God
Patrick shows the Irish three petals on one cloverleaf
Heloise says obedience, chastity, and Abelard constitute one
      lament
Abelard finds ambiguous verbs reside in one Name
Bernard says don't break the Rock into pebbles—You're not
      my brother

2.
Council is over and though the nature
of the Trinity has been settled, flat daylight
follows everyone as before. It sidles
along rooftops and down streets glutted
with mud and sewage, it illuminates
the peddler girl's blush when a young cleric
hands her two coins. Sun dapples the stiff
rumps of the suckling pigs sold next to
sausages. It follows the bishop
and his bodyguards as they leave
the cathedral and elbow through the market.
Light splatters the purple robe. Heresy

has been found in ink brewed from oak bark.
Sun barely touches the spears, then moves on.

Accompanied only by his philosophy
of God and more soldiers, Peter Abelard
is led to ecclesiastical jail. The crowd hoped
for a hanging—for more than a book to burn.
As a courtesy, the philosopher is not bound
and he tears at a sleeve with one hand,
his eyes fixed on the monastery ahead,
his days to come as a prisoner. Then the scent
of smoking wood and leather reaches him,
confirming his dread. They're burning his child.
The clever one out of Lady Logic, the lovely
cradled in pergamino, adorned with indigo
script. In Brittany the same light crawls weakly
across a room where his other child
wears a cousin's clothes and tries to speak.
His son would say *father,*
would say a word like *love,*
but has no reference.

3.
The flames are not impressive, nor is a single
book of thought pungent as heretic meat.
The sun ambles above unwashed merchants,
smelly customers, noisy priests, and the shrinking
philosopher. The hour wears down. Hawkers' fires
and the bits of flesh they sell win the day. As Abelard
and the soldiers disappear, an old crusader considers
the smouldering book and wonders at the nature
of sin. Though he's been absolved time and again
by one priest and another, he can't forget an aroma.
The infidel babe turned on the spit and his parents
boiled. God's design, he thinks, has many parts.

And so I took myself off to a lonely spot I had known before in the territory
of Troyes, and there built a sort of oratory . . . here I could stay hidden
alone . . .

    Peter Abelard, *Historia calamitatum*

Gibbous Moon
(The Paraclete, on the River Ardusson)

Though he has escaped hanging,
this evening the monk forgets to recite
the prayers. Drinking the day's final gold,
he rests beside a hut of mud and thatch.
Here the Ardusson is less river than
pond. Holding a cup of wine he's blessed
for himself, he regards wood ducks swimming
ahead of the dark towards shore and nest.

The hut pleases him. Its humility
he reads as emblem of a man
given one more life. Here he is hidden,

but barely—in retreat, but near the market
road. Smouldering young *vagantes*
who wax and wane between teacher and
master will find him soon. These earthy
dwellings will multiply, he'll create
an enclave, a school. Scholars
from all Christendom will rekindle
his ruined name and cook for him—
small fee to enter the vast dialogue
that is Peter Abelard's mind. But now
that great chamber of thinking settles

into the hour as if fashioned
of evening itself. The Ardusson's
calm sustains the moon, white
and swollen. From the rushes a momentary
clamour stirs the air as if a clapper
has touched, once, its bell. A trout arcs
above the water to receive its food,
fragmenting the lunar wafer. Even as it breaks,
the moon recomposes. Shapeless
as water, Abelard's thoughts drift along
the dusk. The empty cup inside him fills,
unnoticed, almost to the brim. There floats
the moon also, brief contentment's double.
At the lark's last note and the bat's first
skim above the river, a morsel of poetry
rises to the learned surface
of his memory, *Who falls stood never*
sure. Then it drifts away.

                              Wilderness freed
the desert fathers of words, but now
Abelard shakes off the given water
of this moment. The God he expects
will appear robed in purple syllogism,
speaking measured Latin. And perhaps
He will. River and sky hold that too.

St. Jerome warns us, "It is difficult to preserve modesty at table."
    Letter 5, Heloise to Peter Abelard

My abbot of St. Denis took possession of the Abbey of Argenteuil . . . so that the nuns were now scattered as exiles.
    Peter Abelard, *Historia calamitatum*

Heloise: Expulsion
    (Abbey of Ste. Marie of Argenteuil, 1129)

Somebody covets this piece of land,
our consecrated keep,
our roof. There was the grant, from Charlemagne,
there was parchment, but it's scraped
new of ancient ink.
There must be someone to blame.

"Notorious immorality!"
even the king lends his seal
to the charge. What did I say at table?
The bishops read Ovid,
wealthy visitors desire
conversation with me,
infamous me. And I long to say
his name. Someone listens.

Reputation, nun's scant allure, with a word
turns to infamy. No abbey
wants me. Where shall I sleep? How
to wash this garment
when I own no other?

You taught her not to reason but to fornicate. In one deed you are guilty of many crimes . . .
          Roscelin of Compiègne, Letter to Peter Abelard

I realized that this was an opportunity sent me by the Lord for providing for my oratory.
          Peter Abelard, *Historia calamitatum*

Deed
   (Auxerre, 1131)

Her suspect name racing ahead,
she's travelled for days to stand
with men of rank and vestments.
Some find this meeting amusing,
a footnote to minor scandal. In obedience
to a will not hers, she accepts
title to untilled lands and a chapel of mud.
Sanctuary is her husband's gift,
a job and underlings. Paraclete,
is Third of One and signifies Comfort.

"To my wife
Comfort
In thatch between weather and you
In wall between forest and pallet where you sleep
In the gate latch

Comfort from the river more articulate than we
Year after year water fowl nesting on the bank
May fish to rush to your nets

Comfort in scriptorium and books
My writing table now yours
Comfort in Words the last and the first

In a chapel with three panes of waxed cloth
The wound at centre
Comfort in Spirit as I swear the Spirit succours me

Comfort and a staunch for this attachment of yours
Bloated like a moon—
Some peace for me."

As the legate holds aloft the deed
writ on lamb's skin scraped fine, light
behind him illumes the script. Witnesses
nod, one lifts an eyebrow. Man and wife
decline to look at each other.
                              Hot wax,
signet ring: the rest of her days
meet her in the imprimatur of Abbess.
Here ravels out the final strand
in a fiction she's woven and cloistered—

Lover so absent, chevalier, returns
to her bed. He tears away the veil,
then leads her past a gate. They enter
the deep, wide night. There, eager
to bear them, the great horse stamps.

At your urgent request, my sister Heloise, once dear to me in the world, now dearest in Christ, I have written what are called 'hymns' in Greek, 'tehillim' in Hebrew.
Letter 4, Peter Abelard to Heloise

Heloise: Hymns

Our daughters praise you.
All winter icy splinters of song
rose towards the chapel's rough
planed rafters and scrolled
your lambent phrases upon them.

Your Christ-filled logic ignited
the space around the Paraclete,
our burden, your praise.
We had hours yet to toil and hard
prayers under our knees.

We had no money, and for barter
nothing. Sister knelt
before sister wrapping
her feet in rags. No fire to counter
the altar's bulk. But desire
grew silently. Squatter in every corner,
it pried open locks to chambers
beneath our veils.

As I slept, winter's insatiable
form moved over me. I woke
pinioned by the rough habit
you've dressed me in.

Spring brought melt and a low priest
to confess us. The daughters in Christ
sang, and the priest remarked
our fortune. After prayers,
your hymns stayed in the chapel,
fading with smoke and sputter of candle fat.
Here poetry is an alien.
The sisters thank you.

*What a hateful loss and grievous misfortune if you had abandoned
yourself . . . to bear in suffering a few children for the world . . .*
Letter 4, Peter Abelard to Heloise

Astralabe: Infidel

(Le Pallet, Brittany)

It is 1126 and the game boys play is Crusade. My cousin will
inherit this courtyard and won't need schooling. So, appropriate
to our futures, he plays Templar. I am Astralabe the Infidel.

A monk at the gate! His skin is dusty as a donkey's. I think he is
a phantom and a thief. He clutches a heavy book to his chest.
It weighs more than I would. Stop! Who pushes me against this
monk? Does he know me? Yes. Here my seasons end.

He mutters a few words in church tongue, *filius*. My stern aunt
greets him. He sits at our table but speaks little and has no
prayer for us. He sleeps by the fire and leaves before light. Later
she shows me the book, "You will master this. You will see me
turn away."

The Infidel wears scarlet and rides a war-horse. He slaughters
the landed knights from Brittany and the priests. He curses our
True God and he will prevail.

O Give thanks unto the Lord, for he is good: because his mercy endureth forever.

Psalms, 118.1

Correction must therefore be rigorous, to the extent that any sister who has seen something to be corrected in another and concealed it shall be subjected to a harsher discipline than the offender.

Letter 7, Peter Abelard to Heloise

Heloise: Terce

This is our business, God
and nun. On backless benches
under east windows beaten
hot by the sun, sisters face
sisters. Benedict has told us
to a fool words mean
nothing. Thus we count out
each other's sins, mighty,
yet easy to forget. We must not
fear the rod.
Even if toothless and old,
we must not fear:
we love one another.

Heloise: Sext

Today when the hour drones
it means only bell.
Over the field clouds swell
but none invite erotic

thought. The habitual drink
at meal tastes not sweet,
not sharp.
Like a crackled wineskin,

my heart.
It can hold a little yet.

I am gone like the shadow when it declineth.
        Psalms, 109.23

Heloise: Vespers

Our mouths spill the litany, tolling
to the forest's rim. She approaches our walls.

We don't hear what summons her.
We wear veils and are married to God.

The setting sun burnishes her flanks. My sisters
turn their backs. The doe is my sister.

Her bed is soft pine needles, her scent autumn
and tree bark and oestrus. I would go with her.

Beyond the convent's measured garden and seamed fields
stand the woods. Hours yet to compline.

Is she my sister?

My habit loosens, prayer book and key fall.
The ground is warm. Twigs avoid my bare feet.

Near the forest gate others wait. I hear their barks.
They are home in moonlight. Hoofs glint.

The stag!

Then, between me and glade stand the cherubim.
Sword burns my lips and the babble begins.

Small words for sister, for words,
for doe vanished in the dark.

You went on to your old perpetual complaint against God concerning the
manner of our entry into religious life.
> Letter 4, Peter Abelard to Heloise

Astralabe: Letters of Direction,
or My Mother Makes a Go of It

Stop beating this tired horse, he tells my mother (in so many
words). Think of all I have given you, Sister in Christ, all I have
given! As your servant, take the body pierced, take this abbey
made of stone and regeneration, daughters dressed for dying,
take your title; praise your life. "Farewell, Bride of Christ," he
writes, "Live in Christ."

But wait! She Who Asks Great Questions for Him, She Who
Knows He Loves to Answer spins her quill. But wait! Don't stop
writing! We weak-minded women have questions. Where did
this idea of nuns come from? How can Benedict's law fit our
moist bodies? What should we wear next to our skin? And what
if a man sits at our table where wine is drunk with enjoyment?
Or if the queen on her way to a Crusade appears at our gate,
curious to see what comes of passion, how silent should we
be?

She's caged in a convent, and he quotes Timothy to her: "I do
not permit a woman to be a teacher. She should be quiet." And
he's telling her that the abbess "whose care is for spiritual rather
than material matters, must not leave her convent." And she
reads the letters she's asked him to write, and hasn't she always
been an obedient dove?

Still, given time, the features in her secreted mirror shift and adapt to another species. The mask of sacrificial pigeon she has groomed to wear through every door begins to acquire a definite curve to the beak. Like a Minerva bird's, her neck muscles learn to swivel and see many sides. She grows agile.

Because she is a Daughter of Logic, she begins to assess the Paraclete. To make a go of it, a small abbey in Champagne needs fields, granaries, mills, cattle, forests, pigs, and lay brothers or peasants at the crops, many lay brothers or peasants at task. An entire hamlet would be useful, a tannery too. How is her virgin-again womb to spring forth daughters and endowments?

At last, she's lucky in something. The times are with her. It's 1130 and women's monastery is a growth industry: Like a new broom, celibacy is sweeping through the Church. Affluent clerics need to find their concubines a place to live. Husbands want rid of wives, wives of means don't want husbands, fathers with a covey of daughters discover the church dot cheaper than a marriage dowry. And how can I explain the mothers— the epidemic of mothers—who leave their children and enter a convent to pray for the Christ Child? Then, there's my class of the population—little bastards almost well born who, like the concubines, need to be stored somewhere respectable and remote.

But Heloise needs a gimmick, a draw. Clever Petronilla at Fontevauld who boards royal women and reformed whores, counts fifty chapter houses and who-knows-how-many acres. At St. Rupert's on the Rhine, Hildegard of the Visions writes operas and encourages her nuns to be creative with headwear. The Mourning Dove of the Paraclete takes stock of her capital, which is her biography and a woman's rogue desire to read. My mother finds a good mare for herself and a serviceable one for the requisite companion. The Count in Provins keeps a good table (venison, wine, banter) and he has surplus daughters, aunts, nieces.

Though she's got a property suit against him, Bernard of Clair-vaux, nemesis of my father, is invited to say mass and eat a meatless meal. He splatters barley soup on his white robe and finds her recommendable. So her enterprise builds, daughter house after daughter house, patchwork of properties and hamlets.

Mother of Many Daughters, Mother of Invisible Son, Mother of No Family, her glamour holds! The vaguely noble, the new rich, the medieval bluestockings flock to the well-run nest and heady classes of Heloise, sister avian to the cardinal and purple of her species.

Peter Abelard proves by his life, by his behaviour and by his books . . . he looks like a monk on the outside, but inside he is a heretic.

Bernard of Clairvaux, Trial at Sens of Abelard
for heresy, 1140

Astralabe: Ordeals

Bishops in bruise-coloured robes and a splatter of cardinals meet in the Cathedral of Sens to condemn my father for heresy. It's high ecclesiastical drama. Young King Louis attends and brings along glamorous Eleanor who wears a bounty of jewels. Well before evening mass and royal dinner, there should be a resolution.

They have options for his punishment. There are always options. There's ordeal of water. My father can be bound and trussed like a pig for market, his mouth stuffed with pages from his offensive books. Men of God will then throw him into a deep pond to demonstrate Christian logic: if he floats, Satan buoys him; if innocent, he will sink, received by the Holy Spirit. *Deus deorum.*

This has been said, and this. Implication thus. Heresy is a contagion begging for ordeal of fire. In the church square soldiers have had their eyes on the anchor chain for binding him to the stake. It will be shown that a heretic is falsely brave when he accepts the chain. The heretic does not cry when he sees the hillock of wood stacked about him. Nor when it is lit. As for the repentant, fire clears his head. *Quam bonum.*

There is the ordeal of stone. My father can be laid upon a table like a main course, and in the charity of Christ, brothers who love him and grieve for his soul will press stone upon stone upon his chest, freeing him of onerous heretical breath. How iron must be his bones, how like stone his own heart to bear such love? *Confitemini Domino.*

This has been said. That. Therefore. Hanging will clot heresy in the blasphemer's throat.

And there is the ordeal of silence. Locked with him in the prison cell of my father's mind, Spirit will hound him with a cacophony of unutterable proofs. *Beati immaculate.*

But silence is my father's reply. His words, his only wealth, are degraded in the mouths of yammerers. *When the charges began to be read out, Abelard refused to listen and walked out.*

He walks out of the cathedral because
1—He is ill and has lost his bearings.
2—He's still a fox, and will appeal the unheard case in Rome.
3—Christ refused to answer Pilate.

My father chooses the ordeal of life. The heretic and the honest man make their own paths. My father who is old and disoriented will walk to Rome. On dusty roads he will leave prints of his swollen feet and discarded propositions, on sharp little stones smears of his blood.

My father has a train of followers who walk with him. But, as things in life go, esprit de corps begins to fade—too many unfriendly messengers pass, riding to and from Rome. Soon only one is left with him. The one he does not remember. Father, I tell him, I will guide you to a door that opens.
Confitemini Domino.

Then let that morning come, as come it will
When this disguise I carry shall be no more.

Ovid, *The Metamorphoses*, XV

Silence Perpetual
(Abbey of Cluny, Burgundy)

silence
pen and voice still

body confined to a cell
one courtyard, one mass

silence
in the grand library

shifting bars of light
slip hours across his desk

silence
through the sieve of his thought

flow grand names
their power like dreams

ideas lift and return to him
lift and repeat

his mind is a water wheel
turning in a dam

into the silence
fall fragments of chant

at night fireflies drift
untouchable

silence
the gift

Logic has made me hated by the world.
    "Confession of Faith" Peter Abelard to Heloise

With you night is splendid day.
    Man to Woman, Letter 22, *Lost Love Letters*

Abelard: Confession, to Heloise

And so, to banish fearful anxiety and all uncertainties
from the heart within your breast, receive assurance from me . . .

I confess you made night glorious day
and each dawn I left your bed was dark falling.

I confess I was born to a first son's claims,
but rejected the life of merely a man.

For I believed God's mind to be
a crystal of logic, every syllogism

something of its core. And even if
I opened a small window of thought,

I confess blindness to prisms. Lady, I am shamed
before Christendom and orphaned to the world.

I admit relentless pursuit of Lady Philosophy,
and I confess a false loyalty to you.

Because I mistook the nature of Truth,
Before you I confess my ignorance.

But I spoke truth to name you Helios, Sun.

A woman comes here to sit beside me.
She wears white linen and her face is yours.

I am finished with words, and confess
each day without you has been dark falling.

Wherever my body may lie, buried or unburied, I beg you have it brought
to your burial ground where . . . Our sisters in Christ may see my tomb.
Letter 2, Peter Abelard to Heloise

Heloise: Return

The seasons had done their work: rid me
of teeth and blessed you with the bride
named Presence.

Two mules pulled your coffin from Chalon.
The Venerable rode beside you,
bearing our new respectability in a letter. Prodigal
at my gate, your bed was ready.

Our daughters saw to it the Abbot was fed.

Narcissus loved the image that he thought was shadow . . .
    Ovid, *Metamorphoses*, III

Heloise: Pond of Seeing
  (Convent of the Paraclete)

Face to face with the woman in the water,
I met again the foible and misstep,
the street singing, ballad and dirge.

Met her who had pushed me down the stair
to a public cell, each day a small turning
in the locked ending. I love you, thought

the one who gazed back at me. Here was
the stranger to feed, wound wanting
balm. Here the image to carry across the final

bridge. Here the oblation wrapped in fine cloth
that I will lay upon the other shore.

Better is the end of a thing than the beginning thereof.
  Ecclesiastes, 7.8

Heloise: Companion

Spaniel soul,
the hawk's shadow covers us.
Yet you run to the river
as if the feeding drake
calls you, or the water bug
that journeys into a dark
throat. You bark at the water wheel.

Beside the bank you crouch and memorize,
I think, messages in summer reeds
as they submit to the wind.

Fidgety companion, at vigils
the night jar's clack
makes you start then cry
outright. In the owl's quaver
we hear time leading on.

Hungry little distraction,
your panting worries me,
the incessant hunt
wearies. Let us sit here,
like friends, touching,

faces to sun and river,
backs to the built wall.

Quiet now, little soul,
heart off-key,
there's a journey yet,
and for sustenance
we have but each other.

Early will I seek thee: my soul thirsts for thee, my flesh longs for thee in a dry and thirsty land.
Psalms, 63.1

Lauds

frugal candle
lights the chapel vault

sleepy nuns too dull
for thought
sing their labour

on the wall one figure
quavers

this is the song
that pours like water
from stone

Heloise, Our Mother Abbess
16 May 1163, Necrology of The Paraclete

Escape

For days the abbess falls
from tyranny of a wakeful
body, tedium of spooned

sustenance. At last someone lays
the final linen over her face
and she steps onto a plain

etched vivid with grasses. Nearby
a girl ambles, waiting. Her hair
is loose. The old woman hears

a man's voice, distant
but approaching. Around her
silence billows, grand and

blue. What did it matter,
after all? A strand of hair teases
her cheek, or it's the welcome of dust.

You are buried inside my breast for eternity . . .
    Man to Woman, Letter 22, *Lost Love Letters*

Heloise: Three Days' Space

This is the legend.
The sisters wrap me in a wedding shroud,
then open your tomb. Twenty years
we have waited, you're holding out
your arms. You pull me to your breast.
Clods of dirt rain down but turn,
as they touch us, to fragrant petals.

Not so.
It was death like any other.
They carried me to a new cell. Side by side
our coffins stand in the crypt. Like beds
in a stone orphanage, they never touch.
Nor do our worn-out bones.

The descent took three days and hymns
composed by Peter Abelard. My old nuns,
soft as pillows, chose the songs.

La très sage Heloise, seduced yet again.

Him . . . God cherishes in his bosom, and keeps him there to be restored to you through His grace . . .
  Letter 115, Peter the Venerable to Heloise

Heloise: Life After, I

Finding you was easy, after
the three-day crossing. As if desire
had created you, waiting on the pier,

arms outstretched. How the wind lifts
these spaces, dislocates, and never
changes! We have rooms, meadows, even

cliffs looking to England. Light assumes
alabaster qualities when we love. Yet, too long
gazing into your eyes buckles the walls

and rends the veil of heaven.
This is but one chamber
in the Mighty Heart. Just out of reach,

you stand at the centre of a grand hall,
or stroll with companions in philosophical
groves. Like leaves in May your words

shimmer. *Yes,* the sages nod. I know them,
these minds. Their discourse sates
your desire. You and I once recited

litanies of their names. And the Other
is there, as well, the Ghost Lit Within
who took me, but loves you. This curtain

of seeing will never close. Your ghost
beside me is nothing but ghost. Dust,
this life after, no different from the first.

Nor have the years in furthest reach of time / Made things turn dust in your bright memory.

Ovid, *Metamorphoses*, XV

Astralabe: Life After, II

Night poor, you readers to come will never know the deep medieval darkness of sky. Never consult the sagacity of stars, nor walk companionably with us. Oracles all, we glinter and spin, even if we've fallen from sight.

You pursuers of charts and genealogies, where will you find the shape of an untold myth? Where in the constellations of begats are David's abandoned sons, the daughters out of Zeus never counted? We're the ghostly configurations farther back in the night, background whimpers, secondary tales in your telescopes.

When some force decrees, my famous parents pass nearby. Trussed in starry lion skins, still pulling the heavenly chariot. Centuries of cosmic winds have stiffened their extravagant manes, their clawed footprints dissolve in milky dust. Harnessed to her blame, his innocence, they will forever proclaim the doctrine of intention.

But they have given up on metaphors of stars and such. Like an estranged couple reunited, they are charitable with each other, and kindly refrain from touch.

From time to time, my mother nods to me, a few lines discarded from her story. We acknowledge our family name which is Abandoned.

Chosen by some careless god.

Heloise: Life After, III

Not the heaven foretold.
Not resumed romance.

No forgiving children, no contrite
parents. No greeting saints.

But a vast river. A diastole
of crystal. Shiver

and release of light.
At times a shoal

will flicker and bevel.
And it is remembrance, image,

glassy ember.
Then the current folds

and lifts again, restores
the one unfurling. Not what was

foretold, yet it is here
in stars flung into the flow.

We are psalms sung,
the night's shimmer, the air's hum.

Dwelling in these tides,
of boundaries we are free.

Chronology

c.1117   Abelard takes lodging in Fulbert's house and seduces Heloise. The "Lost Love Letters" correspondence begins.

c.1118   Abelard abducts Heloise and sends her to Le Pallet where she bears their son Astralabe. Abelard and Heloise are married in a secret but legal ceremony in Paris, but do not live together. Abelard sends Heloise to the convent at Argenteuil where she wears a nun's habit but not the veil. Fulbert has Abelard castrated. On Abelard's orders Heloise takes the veil at Argenteuil, and he becomes a monk at the Abbey of St. Denis.

1121   Abelard's *Theologia* is condemned and burned at the Council of Soissons.

1122   Abelard founds a hermitage dedicated to the Paraclete.

c.1125–c.1133 Abelard is Abbot at St. Gildas du Rhuys in Brittany

1129   Heloise is Prioress at Argenteuil. Abbot Suger of St. Denis claims the land of Argenteuil and has the convent disbanded. When Heloise and other nuns are not received elsewhere, Abelard establishes them at the Paraclete.

1131   Pope Innocent II grants the charter for the Paraclete, thus taking Heloise and her nuns under papal protection.

c.1132   Abelard's autobiography *Historia calamitatum* appears. The famous correspondence between Abelard and Heloise begins.

1133   Abelard returns to Paris and is a master at Mont-Sainte-Genevieve.

1140   Abelard is accused of heresy by Bernard of Clairvaux at the Council of Sens. Abelard begins walking to Rome to put his case personally before the Pope. Midway in his journey he learns that Pope Innocent II sentences him to perpetual silence as a heretic. At this point Peter the Venerable offers Abelard protection at Cluny and declares him readmitted to "apostolic grace." However, the sentence of silence remains in effect until his death.

c.1142   Abelard dies at the Cluniac house of St. Marcel near Chalon-sur-Saône. The Paraclete establishes its first daughter house.

c.1144   Peter the Venerable personally returns Abelard's body to the Paraclete.

1147   A papal letter confirms all the possessions acquired by the Paraclete since its foundation.

c.1147–63 The Paraclete establishes five daughter houses.

1164   Heloise dies at the Paraclete. At the time of her death, the most popular girl's name in the region is Heloise. The Order of the Paraclete continues for six hundred years.

1789   During the French Revolution, the Order of the Paraclete is dissolved. Apparently most of its documents are destroyed.

Notes

All section epigraphs are from Ovid, *The Metamorphoses*.

Page No.

26 Exposure of unwanted infants was common throughout Europe until the late Middle Ages. The Parthenian Hill figures in numerous classical myths.

28 In the Middle Ages, the *trivium* was the accepted course of liberal arts study. It consisted of Latin rhetoric, classical Latin literature, and logic.

29 A close is the enclosed space of an abbey or cathedral where the pertaining buildings and residences are located.

38 In *The Metamorphoses*, the maiden Io, after being raped by Jove, is turned into a white cow.

39 In *The Metamorphoses*, to ensure that Hippomenes will win the race against Atalanta and therefore wed her, Aphrodite tosses three golden balls in the maiden's path to distract her.

41 There is an unsubstantiated tradition that Abelard is the Arch Poet of the *Carmina Burana*.

43 Quote from *Historia calamitatum*.

48 Robert de Lasteyrie in a study of documents related to a topographical history of Paris (1887) quotes the preamble to the charter turning over the Convent of St. Eloi to the monks of St. Peter-Fossa: *[The nuns of St. Eloi] fell to such great misery of turpitude, arrogantly adhering to open secularism, their vows of chastity broken* . . . Most likely the monks destroyed all the documents of the dissolved St. Eloi or re-used the parchments. For speculation about Hersinde and St. Eloi, see Cook.

50 Le Pallet was the family home of Abelard near Nantes in Brittany.

55 In *Historia Calamitatum* Abelard says he thought himself "The world's philosopher." The word Abelard can be translated as "Licker of Lard" (Clanchy).

60 Between Scylla and Charybdis: in Greek myth, these were two dangerous female sea monsters who lived opposite each other on a narrow strait where ships had to pass. In the twelfth century the phrase "to fall into Scylla while avoiding Charybdis" meant to expose oneself to a danger while avoiding another. Abelard uses this phrase in his "Confession of Faith" letter to Heloise.

63 Quote from *Historia calamitatum*.

70 In *Historia calamitatum* Abelard relates that Heloise quoted these lines from Lucan's *Pharsalia* as she took the veil.

75 In the poems of canonical hours, the epigraphs are scriptural fragments taken from a prescribed reading for that hour, according to the Rule of Benedict. Compline, also called night song, is the hour just before retiring.

76 Vigils is the first hour, around midnight.

77 Prime, or morning song, is around sunrise.

78 The subject of *Theologia*, the book burned at Soissons, was the nature of the Trinity.

81 Italics quoted from Boethius, 480–542 CE.

82 In expelling the nuns from Argenteuil, Abbot Suger of St. Denis argued they had no legal claim to the land, and, for good measure, he accused them of "notorious immorality."

83 November 28, 1131, Pope Innocent II issued a letter from Auxerre confirming the transfer.

88 Terce is the canonical hour at mid-morning. This is when the monastery would hold chapter meeting to discuss business and administer discipline.

89 Sext is the office read at noon to the monastic community as it has its noonday meal.

90 Vespers, or Evensong, is the canonical hour at sunset.

92 Letters 5–7 in the correspondence of Peter Abelard and Heloise deal with her requests for guidance in administering a monastery for women and his replies to her. They are generally called "Letters of Direction."

96   *"When the charges, etc."* quoted from St. Bernard's letters.

99   After Sens, Innocent III burned Abelard's books in a ceremony at St. Peter's and condemned him to perpetual silence and imprisonment in a "place of religion." Peter the Venerable of Cluny gave Abelard refuge and made him a brother of the order.

101   Italics from *Confession of Faith* by Peter Abelard.

107   Lauds is the service sung before dawn.

109   Title comes from "Good Tuesday," a hymn written by Abelard.

Suggested Reading

In writing historical fiction, the author imposes thoughts upon her characters and causes them to commit acts that might puzzle or even outrage the historical subjects. The voices in these poems present themselves filtered through my own experience and language. I take responsibility for factual inconsistencies and emphasize that all interpretations of this story are mine.

In the spirit of discovery, I invite the reader to explore more about Heloise, Peter Abelard, their times, and medieval life in general.

The principal sources of information regarding the relationship of Abelard and Heloise have traditionally been his autobiography, *Historia calamitatum*, and the letters they exchanged between 1132 and 1140. Recently a medieval manuscript, *Epistolae duorum amantium*, has been reliably identified as excerpts from their earlier "lost love letters." In the past two decades there has been increased scholarly attention given to the figure of Heloise. New interpretations of medieval texts have led to a re-appraisal of the nature of this romance, of Heloise's role in the affair, and of her own intellectual and administrative accomplishments.

Works by Peter Abelard and Heloise:

Abelard, Peter. *"Historia calamitatum."* Trans. Betty Radice. *The Letters of Abelard and Heloise.* London & Baltimore: Penguin, 1974.

Heloise and Peter Abelard. Trans. Betty Radice. *The Letters of Abelard and Heloise.* London & Baltimore: Penguin, 1974.

____. (Attributed). Mews, Constant J. Ed. with trans. by Neville Chiavaroli. *The Lost Love Letters of Heloise and Abelard: Perceptions of Dialogue in Twelfth-Century France.* New York: St. Martin's, 1999.

Other Sources:

Benedict, Saint, Abbot of Monte Cassino. *The Rule of St. Benedict.* Ed. Rev. Timothy Fry. Collegeville, MN: The Liturgical Press, 1981.

Boethius (Anicius Manlius Severinus). *The Consolation of Philosophy.* Trans. V.E.Watts. New York: Penguin, 1969.

Burge, James. *Heloise and Abelard: A New Biography.* New York: Harper-Collins, 2006

Clanchy, Michael T. *Abelard: A Medieval Life.* Oxford: Blackwell, 1998.

Cook, Brenda. "The Birth of Heloise: New Light on an Old Mystery?" (http://abaelard.de/070102newlight.htm.September2000)

Gilson, Étienne, *Heloise and Abelard.* Ann Arbor: The University of Michigan Press, 2000.

Guilbert of Nogent. ed. John Benton. *Self and Society in Medieval France: The Memoirs of Abbot Guibert of Nogent.* Trans. C. C. Swinton Bland. Toronto: University of Toronto Press, 1984.

Mews, Constant J., Chapters 1–5. *The Lost Love Letters of Heloise and Abelard: Perceptions of Dialogue in Twelfth-Century France.* Trans. with Neville Chiavaroli. New York: St. Martin's Press, 1999.

Newman, Barbara. *From Virile Woman to WomanChrist: Studies in Medieval Religion and Literature.* Philadelphia: University of Pennsylvania Press, 1995.

Ovid. (Publius Ovidius Naso) *The Metamorphoses.* Tr. Horace Gregory. New York: Viking, 1958; New York: Mentor/Viking, 1960.

____. *The Art of Love.* In *The Erotic Poems.* Trans. Peter Green. Penguin Classics. London: Penguin Books, 1982.

____. *Heroides.* Trans. Grant Showerman. Cambridge: Harvard University Press, 1977 (first published 1914).

Radice, Betty, trans. "Introduction." *The Letters of Abelard and Heloise.* Harmondsworth: Penguin, 1974.

Waddell, Helen. *The Wandering Scholars*. Ann Arbor: University of Michigan Press, 1990. (First published London: Constable, 1927).

___. "Boethius." Trans. in *More Latin Lyrics*. New York: Norton, 1976.

Wheeler, Bonnie. *Listening to Heloise: The Voice of a Twelfth-Century Woman*. New York: St. Martin's Press, 2000.

Whicher, George F., Ed. and Trans. *The Goliard Poets: Medieval Latin Songs and Satires*. Cambridge, MA: The University Press, 1949.

Works of General Interest about Medieval Society:

Abbott, Elizabeth. *A History of Celibacy*. New York: Scribner, 2000. (First published in Canada by Harper Collins, 1999).

Aries, Phillipe, and Georges Duby, Ed. Trans. Arthur Goldhammer. *A History of Private Life: Vol. II Revelations of the Medieval World*. Cambridge, Mass: The Belknap Press of Harvard University Press, 1988. (First published as *Histoire de la vie privée, vol.2, De l'Europe féodale à la Renaissance*, Editions du Seuil, 1985).

Boswell, John. *The Kindness of Strangers: The Abandonment of Children in Western Europe from Late Antiquity to the Renaissance*. Chicago: The University of Chicago Press, 1998.

Gies, Frances and Joseph Gies. *Life in a Medieval Village*. New York: HarperPerennial, 1981

___. *Life in a Medieval City*. New York: HarperPerennial, 1991.

___. *Marriage and the Family in the Middle Ages*. New York: Harper & Row, 1989.

Lacey, Robert, and Danny Danziger. *The Year 1000: What Life Was Like at the Turn of the First Millennium: An Englishman's World*. Boston: Little, Brown and Company, 1999.

Le Goff, ed. Trans. Lydia G. Cochrane. *Medieval Callings*. Chicago: University of Chicago Press, 1990. (First published as *L'uomo medievale*, Rome: Gius, Laterza & Figli Spa, 1987).

McCall, Andrew. *The Medieval Underworld*. New York: Barnes & Noble, 1993.

Power, Eileen. ed. M.M. Postan. *Medieval Women*. Cambridge: Cambridge University Press. 1995. (First published 1975).

Stiller, Nikki. *Eve's Orphans: Mothers and Daughters in Medieval English Literature*. Westport: Greenwood Press, 1980.

Wheeler, Bonnie. *Medieval Heroines in History and Legend*. (Audio). Chantilly, Va: The Teaching Company, 2002.

William, Marty, and Anne Echols. *Between Pit and Pedestal: Women in the Middle Ages*. Princeton: Markus Wiener Publishers, 1994.

Printed in the United States
127756LV00001B/4/P